Ticking Time Bombs

Write like an Author – Course Book Four

Brian Falkner

Falkner Books
2016

This edition published in 2016 by

Falkner Books

Copyright © 2016 by Brian Falkner

Illustrations by Ron Leishman
Some images in this publication used under 'Fair Use' for educational purposes

On the web at:
brianfalkner.com
writelikeanauthor.com

All rights reserved. This book or any portion thereof may not be reproduced or used in any manner whatsoever without the express written permission of the publisher except for the use of brief quotations in a book review or scholarly journal.

First Printing: 2016

ISBN 978-0-9944567-3-1

What if I told you...

...that somewhere in the pages of this book was a secret that would earn you a million dollars.

You'd keep reading, right? You'd avidly turn each page trying to find the secret.

And if I told you that only the first person to find it would win it and it hasn't been found yet, then you'd go all out, reading and re-reading every page, desperate not to miss out on your chance at a million dollars.

That in a nutshell is the difference between **suspense** and **tension**.

Suspense is when there is something you want to know, and you must wait to find out. Tension is how badly you want to find out.

And the funny thing is, if you write a really good book which is full of suspense and high tension for the reader, you just might sell a million copies and earn your million dollars!

Read on, if you dare, to find out how to create heart-stopping suspense and terrifying tension in your stories.

Happy writing!

Brian

BRIAN SAYS

I don't consider myself to be a particularly good writer. Not compared to many of the other wonderful New Zealand and Australian authors I have had the pleasure to meet and to read.

I honestly think the reason for my success, here and around the world, has been my ability to hold the reader in a state of suspense.

That's something I have always known how to do. I learned it by reading many suspenseful books when I was young.

When I because a professional author I needed to study suspense and tension. To analyse them, and understand them more fully.

What I learned by doing that is in this book.

Suspense

Movie director Alfred Hitchcock described suspense like this.

"If you have a scene where two characters are conversing in a cafe, and a bomb suddenly goes off under the table, the audience experiences surprise."

"On the other hand, if the audience sees the saboteur place the bomb, is told that it will go off at one o'clock, and can see a clock in the scene, the mundane conversation between two cafe patrons now becomes one of intense suspense, as the audience holds its collective breath waiting for the explosion."

When the audience (the reader) is waiting for something, wanting to know what will happen, or wanting the answer to a question, they are in a state of suspense.

Suspense keeps readers glued to the page, as long as it goes hand in hand with tension and pacing.

This suspense is terrible.
I hope it will last.
- Oscar Wilde

HITCHCOCK

Alfred Hitchcock was a British film director famous for his suspenseful movies, including:

Dial M for Murder

North by Northwest

Rear Window

Psycho

The Birds

Vertigo

Strangers on a Train

Notorious

The Lady Vanishes

The 39 Steps

Tension

Suspense is essential to a story. But by itself it's not enough. To really have an impact on the reader, it needs to go hand in hand with *tension*.

BRIAN SAYS

It doesn't matter if your story is an action thriller...

Suspense is created by making the reader *wait for something*. Tension is created by *raising the stakes*.

Imagine you are a tightrope walker, carefully stepping along a wire you have strung between two trees in your back yard. You are new to this, so you have strung the wire about knee height.

There is suspense. Will you make it? But there is little tension because you won't hurt yourself if you fall.

...a love story...

Now let's say you string the wire 4 metres up in the air. That increases the tension because the stakes are now higher. If you fall, you might break an arm or a leg.

Let's ramp it up some more. What if the wire was strung across a ravine, 200 metres deep. Now if you fall you will die. Higher stakes, higher tension.

...or a heart-felt drama about a dying dog...

Want even more tension? Ok, you are carrying a baby!

Here's an actual example from my book *The Super Freak*.

- One of the characters climbs a high voltage power pylon.
- It's raining.
- The hero climbs after him.
- There is thunder and lightning.
- The lightning is getting closer.

With each step the tension increases a little bit more.

...you still need suspense and tension.

The higher the stakes, the greater the tension!

Pacing

All the suspense and tension in the world won't help your story if the reader doesn't feel as though they are moving towards the answer or the resolution.

BRIAN SAYS

On the next page I have put an excerpt from *Battlesaurus: Rampage at Waterloo*.

it is deliberately slow paced to enhance the feelings of apprehension and fear.

How quickly the story moves in that direction is called *pace*.

If you intrigue the reader with a question, but pages and pages later there is still no sign of getting any closer to the answer, they could be bored, and may stop reading.

On the other hand, if you intrigue them, then solve the mystery straight away, then there is no time for suspense or tension.

Sometimes you want a fast pace, with lots of things happening quickly. Other times you slow the pace down, deliberately. This can be to give the reader a break, a rest, between long passages of action and tension. Or it can be to create suspense.
Consider these two ways of telling the same events:

> I walked down the hallway and opened the door.

That's quite fast-paced. Let's try it slow paced, to create suspense.

> I stepped into the hallway, scanning both ways for any sign of danger. There was none. The doorway at the end of the hallway was shut, and after some hesitation I took one careful step in that direction. The floorboards creaked....

You get the idea. Slowing the pace can enhance the tension.

Battlesaurus - Ruien Scene

The tunnel finally comes to an end, opening out into a small circular underground lake filled with brackish, sludgy water, and topped with a low dome. In the centre is a wide brick column that holds up the ceiling. Willem can see no exit from the lake, but there is no other way to go, so they wade into the pool. Several times something brushes against Willem's legs and he thinks of eels or something much worse. But whatever it is, it is either uninterested or afraid.

They reach the central brick column and circle around it, dimly seeing the mouth of a tunnel on the far side.

The dome that is the sky above the lake starts to darken as they cross and Francois says, "The lamp!"

The flame has been getting lower and lower as they have crossed the lake, and is now almost gone. With that understanding Willem realizes that he is struggling to breathe. His lungs are working harder and faster yet he feels as though he is suffocating.

"Hurry," he manages to say a voice that is just a hoarse whisper. "No oxygen."

They try to move faster, wheezing and gasping for air, although their footsteps are sluggish in the pond-water which at times seems as thick as treacle.

Jack, guiding his lieutenant, has taken the lead, but Frost stops suddenly, holding up his hand for silence. Willem can barely see it, so low is the flame, and almost collides with them. He hears Heloise and Francois come to a halt behind him.

Frost says nothing, but then they hear what he has heard. The sound of movement. The soft rattle of spines.

A demonsaurus has just entered the lake.

The lamp is so low as to be invisible, but still Willem covers it, quickly, but silently. He is again acutely conscious of the loud sound of his breathing in the thin air.

There is complete silence apart from the sound of the demonsaurus's breathing, laboring in the unbreathable atmosphere. They hear each footstep as it circles them, hunting in the blackness.

Bright spots have appeared inside Willem's eyelids and his head is beginning to waver. There is a slight noise in front of him and he realizes that Frost has slumped over, to be caught by Jack's strong arms.

Still the demonsaurus circles, hunting by feel in a place where all its other senses are useless. It is close now. So close in front of him that he could reach out and touch it.

Willem can feel his head spinning and knows he is losing control, losing consciousness and there is no way he can bear it any long.

Then with a series of splashing footsteps the creature is gone, like the humans, unable to stay in a place with no oxygen.

BATTLESAURUS

To put this scene in context, our heroes are desperately trying to escape from Belgium and sail to England.

The only way to bypass Napoleon's forces is underground, through the *'Ruien'* the old sewer system of Antwerp.

Unfortunately the French are on their tail and release a small vicious 'saur' into the tunnels behind them: a creature they call a 'demonsaur'.

Our heroes carry a miner's lamp that warns them of low oxygen.

Note the deliberately slow pacing of this scene, but the escalating tension as their situation goes from dire to worse.

The Hook

A hook is simply a small piece of information that will make the reader wonder something.

A hook raises a question in the mind of the reader, and doesn't reveal the answer.

The hook is often used in opening lines of stories.

Opening Lines Quiz

Can you name the book from the opening line? But more importantly, can you spot the hook, hidden in the words?
Clue: One of the books is mine.

1. All children, except one, grow up

2. "Where's Papa going with that axe?" said Fern to her mother as they were setting the table for breakfast.

3. When the doorbell rings at three in the morning, it's never good news.

4. If you are interested in stories with happy endings, you would be better off reading some other book.

5. There is no lake at Camp Green Lake.

6. When Maddy started speaking Japanese, her mum took her to the doctor.

7. I felt her fear before I heard her screams.

8. It was almost December, and Jonas was beginning to be frightened.

9. Look, I didn't want to be a half-blood.

10. He began his new life standing up, surrounded by cold darkness and stale, dusty air.

MY STORY

Here are some ideas that I have been trying out for my opening line. Which one do you think works best to draw the reader into the story?

The police officers were polite and sympathetic. But sympathy would not bring back my baby sister.

From the outside it appeared to be just an ordinary apartment building.

"When was the last time you saw your sister alive?"

Had I know what I was getting myself into I would never have left the apartment.

She was only four. Somehow that makes it all worse.

The Hook - Exercise

Use this sheet to rewrite the opening line of a well-known story. Include an attention grabbing hook.

Use one of these stories:

Once upon a time, there was a little girl who lived in a village near the forest. Whenever she went out, the little girl wore a red riding cloak, so everyone in the village called her Little Red Riding Hood...

(Little Red Riding Hood)

Once upon a time, there was a little girl named Goldilocks. She went for a walk in the forest...

(Goldilocks and the three Bears)

Once upon a time in a land much like yours and mine lived a young girl named Ella. She was born in a small house with her mother, Lily, and her father, a hardworking merchant...

(Cinderella)

MY LINE

I am going to do this exercise with Jack and the Beanstalk.

Here is the original opening line:

Once upon a time, there lived a widow woman and her son, Jack, on their small farm in the country.

And here is my version:

Jack would never have known that the bean was magic if his mother hadn't thrown it out of the window.

Write your opening line here:

Foreshadowing

To foreshadow something in a story is to give a glimpse of something that will happen in the future.

Usually it is something horrible, or wonderful, or frightening or amazing. The reader knows it is going to happen, and can't wait to get there.

Look at this line from my book The Tomorrow Code:

> The end of the world started quietly enough for Tane Williams and Rebecca Richards.

This is an example of foreshadowing. The line lets the reader know that the end of the world is approaching. It foreshadows something that will take place later in the book.

Foreshadowing is not *telegraphing*. That is where you reveal too much of what is to come and ruin the surprise for the reader.
Let me try and illustrate with a simple example, using the Kornfeld story. We never found out what happened after the incident in the story, but let's assume that eventually the narrator and Kornfeld ended up friends.

If I had wanted to foreshadow this, then early in the story I might have written something like this:

> Whatever reasons my olds had for coming to this country, they weren't good enough. These kids and I had nothing in common (except for one, but I didn't know that at the time).

That's a bit clumsy, but it is foreshadowing. It hints at something that is to come. *Telegraphing* might be something like this:

> Kornfeld entered. The last person I would have expected to end up as my best friend.

That gives away too much information and ruins the suspense.

BRIAN SAYS

I recently read a suspense thriller that has been a huge hit world-wide. (I won't name it.) The author used so much foreshadowing that it was driving me crazy.

On almost every page there was a sentence foreshadowing something later in the novel.

If you over-use any suspense technique the reader will start to notice the technique and it will stop being effective.

(Having said that, the book was a world-wide best-seller, so maybe the author had it right!)

Foreshadowing Exercise

Highlight the foreshadowing in each of these examples.

THE BOOKS

> Where do thoughts come from?
> You know, like you're sitting in maths and the teacher is droning on about isosceles triangles and suddenly into your mind pops the thought that you'd really like a big date scone with jam and whipped cream. Which has nothing to do with isosceles triangles.
> Where do thoughts like that come from? I don't know. I'm not a scientist, or a psychologist or anything like that.
> But I do know where some thoughts come from. Like the time that Fuhrer Bluchner in French class wrote "knickers" on the board instead of "naitre". I know where that thought came from. It came from me.
> Perhaps I should explain. My name is Jacob John Smith, and this is the unlikely story of the crime of the century.

> Fizzer Boyd was blessed with E.S.P. Not Extra-Sensory-Perception. Fizzer couldn't read your thoughts, or tell the future. What Fizzer had was Extraordinary Sensory Perception.
> Sight, sound, touch, smell, Fizzer was amazing at them all. But the sense he was most well-known for – that he became world-famous for – was his sense of taste.

> On Friday, on his way to school, Sam Wilson brought the United States of America to its knees.
> He didn't mean to. He was actually just trying to score a new computer and some other cool stuff, and in any case the words "to its knees" were the New York Times' not his. (And way over the top in Sam's view.) Not as bad though as the Washington Post. Their headline writers must have been on a coffee binge because they screamed
>
> ## National Disaster
>
> in size-40 type when their presses finally came back online.
> Anyway it was only for a few days, and it really wasn't a disaster at all. At least not compared to what was still to come.

The Big Secret

To use this technique, you let the reader know that there is a big secret, but you don't reveal the secret until the last possible minute.

In my book *Assault* about an alien invasion of Earth, I let the reader know that the aliens have a secret base inside Uluru (also known as Ayers Rock, it is a vast rock in the middle of the Australian Outback) where they are conducting a secret project that could be devastating for the human race.

The heroes of the story must travel and fight to get inside Uluru. They are desperate to find out the secret and so is the reader. This creates suspense as they go on the journey with the heroes.

In another of my books, *The Project*, the two heroes, Tommy and Luke, discover a very old, very rare, very boring book.

They quickly find out that the book is boring for a reason. It hides a terrible secret that could change the course of history.

Again, the secret is not revealed until the last possible minute.

A word of caution if you intend to use The Big Secret technique in your story.

The secret has to be worth the wait. Your readers will feel very let down if they wait and wait and wait to find out the secret, and when they find it out, they just go 'Meh!'

BRIAN SAYS

Another book that was incredibly successful in recent years was *The Da Vinci Code* by Dan Brown.

It became one of the biggest selling thrillers of all time. I personally didn't enjoy it as much as I wanted to. But I kept reading, page after page. Why? Because it's one of the best examples of the 'Big Secret' technique.

There is a huge secret, but you have to read almost all the way to the end to find out what it is.

And it is worth the wait!

Big Secret Examples

Here are a few books that have a 'Big Secret', Including a couple of mine!

Holes by Louis Sachar

One of my favourite books, and it contains an excellent example of a 'big secret'. Every morning the inmates of a teenage prison camp in the desert have to get up and dig a hole one metre round by one metre deep. Why? That's the secret.

The Maze Runner by James Dashner

What is the secret of the maze?

Harry Potter and the Philosopher's Stone

What is the secret of the scar on Harry's forehead

The Project by Brian Falkner

What is the secret hidden in the most boring book in the world?

Northwood by Brian Falkner

What is the secret of the mysterious Northwood forest?

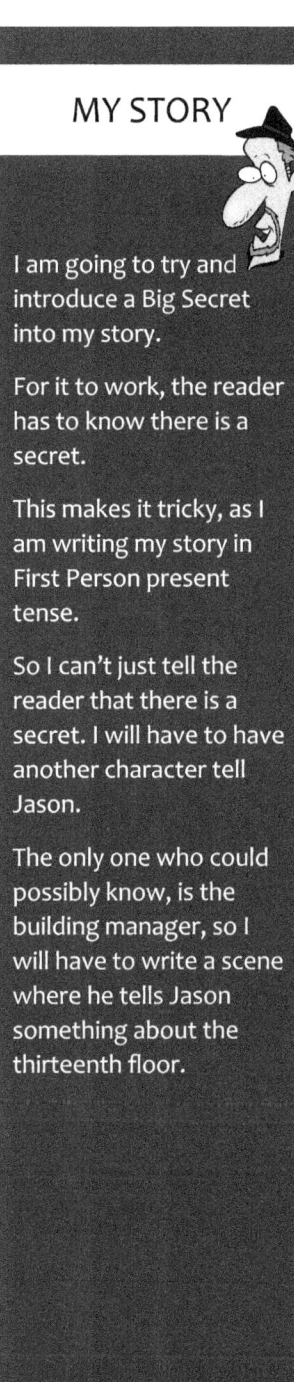

MY STORY

I am going to try and introduce a Big Secret into my story.

For it to work, the reader has to know there is a secret.

This makes it tricky, as I am writing my story in First Person present tense.

So I can't just tell the reader that there is a secret. I will have to have another character tell Jason.

The only one who could possibly know, is the building manager, so I will have to write a scene where he tells Jason something about the thirteenth floor.

Dramatic Irony

Dramatic irony is one of the most effective techniques for creating suspense, and also one of the simplest. You simply let the reader know something the character doesn't know. (The Hitchcock café scene is an example of dramatic irony.)

Consider this scene:

> Morgan quietly opened the door to the corridor and stopped, searching the long dusty hallway for any sign of movement, or trouble. There was none. The rusted metal frame of the doorway at the end of the corridor beckoned to him. He took one careful footstep towards it. The floorboards creaked beneath his shoe.

In this scene the reader and the character have exactly the same information. So let's reveal something to the reader that the character doesn't know.

> The creature waited in silence behind the rusting metal frame of the door. For ten years it had waited, in ever-increasing hunger. Now it smelled blood. Poisonous slime began to drip from its fangs as it continued to wait. Just a little longer.
> Morgan quietly opened the door to the corridor and stopped, searching the long dusty hallway for any sign of movement…

We know there is a monster behind the door, but Morgan doesn't. That puts the reader into a state of suspense.

BRIAN SAYS

Disney movies often use dramatic irony.

Here are a few examples:

The Lion King
The audience knows that Scar killed Mufasa. But Simba thinks he was responsible (because that's what Scar told him). The audience knows more than the character.

Snow White

When the old lady comes to visit Snow White, we know that she is really the evil queen. Worse, we know that the apple she offers Snow White is poisoned.

Frozen

The audience knows that Elsa has powers she cannot control, but Anna does not know this.

Cliff-hangers

Cliff-hangers are a very effective way of keeping the reader glued to the pages of your story.

At the end of a scene or a chapter you leave your character in a precarious situation.

Maybe their life is in danger, or it might be some kind of emotional stress.

Whatever it is, you leave them in danger at the end of the scene or chapter.

If you are writing a short story, there might not be different chapters, but you can still use the cliff-hanger by using different scenes and cutting between points of view (More about that soon).

Here is an actual example of a cliffhanger from my alien invasion book, 'Assault'.

In this scene, a team of six teenager soldiers have just jumped out of an aeroplane over the Australian desert using a kind of parachute system called a 'half-pipe.'

> The pipping stopped. There was a moment's silence, followed by a screech inside his helmet and a red flashing light.
>
> The half-pipe had failed to deploy.
>
> He punched at the manual override. Another screech, and the red light was still blasting at him. His landing gear had failed.
>
> Those panicky hands were back around his heart and nothing was going to persuade them to loosen their grip. Lieutenant Ryan Chisnall of the Allied Combined Operations Group, Reconnaissance Battalion, was now falling toward the barren Australian desert at terminal velocity.
>
> Very terminal.

That's the end of the chapter. Ryan is falling to his certain death. To keep the reader in suspense as long as possible about Ryan's fate, I combine the cliff-hanger with the split point of view.

MY STORY

I'd love to include a cliff-hanger in my story, but it is very difficult in a short story with only one Point of View and no chapters.

For a cliffhanger to work, I would need to leave Jason in danger at the end of a chapter or scene.

I will think about cheating on the Point of View, and maybe having a few scenes from Charli's point of view, or maybe from his mother's.

I will have to be very careful about this, because it is important to be consistent with the point of view in a story.

Split Point of View

As we talked about in the Word Warriors workbook, it is important to choose a point of view for the reader. Usually it is the main character's POV that we use.

But often you will alternate scenes between different characters' POV. Sometimes between the hero and the villain. We see what the hero is doing, then what the villain is doing.

At the end of a 'hero' scene you try to leave them in a cliff-hanger situation, keeping the reader in suspense until the next hero scene.

Here is the next chapter in *Assault*. I have switched point of view from Ryan to an 'omniscient' narrator point of view where I can tell the reader stuff. The next chapter in the book starts with a scene where I describe to the reader the way the 'half-pipe' works.

> The High-Altitude Freefall Landing Pad—Personnel was developed in secret by the British military in the early 2010s. The HAFLP-P, commonly known as the "half-pipe," worked off a basic law of physics: it makes no difference whether a human being jumps from 200 feet, or 32,000 feet. After the first few seconds, the human body falls as fast as gravity can make it—terminal velocity. So a stuntman falling from a high building and a skydiver falling from an aircraft would hit the ground at approximately the same speed.
>
> The half-pipe consists of a landing pad made of an incredibly strong but gossamer-thin fabric, and a compressed-air cylinder. When it hits the ground, the half-pipe landing pad inflates instantly, like an airbag in a car, expanding to the size of a swimming pool.
>
> The way to survive the fall is to hit the pad dead center, which is a lot harder to do from 32,000 feet than from 200 feet. From 32,000 feet, even a landing pad the size of a football field would appear as a mere pinprick far below.

This description goes on for a couple of pages, holding the reader in suspense about the fate of Lieutenant Ryan Chisnall.

BRIAN SAYS

A lot of books use the split POV technique. One of my favourites, which does it very effectively, is the second book in the *Lord of the Rings* series: *The Two Towers*.

The point of view switches between Frodo and Sam; Merry and Pippin; Aragorn; and Gimli and Legolas.

Technically this is called an *omniscient* point of view, which is a kind of god-like point of view where you can see everyone and everything.

But it allows us to swap between the different stories, almost always leaving the characters in a cliff-hanger situation.

The other thing you can do by splitting the point of view, is to have different tones.

You can break up a serious or scary scene, by interspersing it with some lighter, or humourous scenes.

High Tension Lines

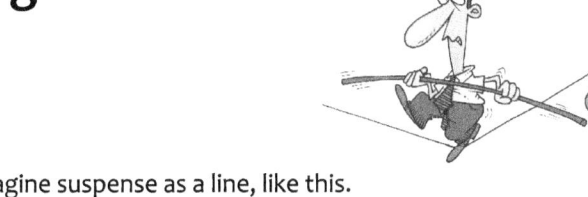

Imagine suspense as a line, like this.

The start of the line is where you raise the question (the hook) and the end of the line is where you let the reader off the hook by giving them the answer. For example:

Ryan is falling without a parachute! (Will Ryan survive?)   Trianne Price reinflates her Half Pipe (Ryan survives!)

While the reader is on the hook they must keep reading, line after line, page after page.

The length of the line shows how long you want to keep the reader in suspense and the thickness of the line represents the amount of tension.

So a long line might depict something like this:

●───────────────────────────────○

Will the hero get the girl?   They fall in love and live happily ever after

That line might go on page after page. But there is little tension. The reader wants to know, but is not on the edge of their seat.

A shorter line with much more tension could be something like this:

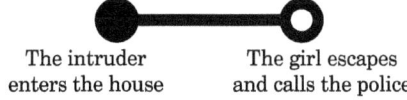

The intruder enters the house   The girl escapes and calls the police

A good rule to follow is that lines of high tension should not go on too long. You should resolve them reasonably quickly. Lower tension can go on much longer.

BRIAN SAYS

The information on this page is probably the most important stuff I am going to tell you about suspense.

By overlapping suspense and tension lines you can keep the reader glued to the page.

If a line ever finishes before you have hooked the reader with one or two more, then there is a real chance of your reader getting away.

Many times while I am reading a book I stop and ask myself, why am I reading right now? What am I dying to find out?

If I don't have an answer to the question, it can be a struggle to continue. However if the suspense is well handled, then I don't even get to ask that question. I am too busy reading!

High Tension Lines

What happens when you let the reader off the hook? This is no longer any suspense or tension and they no longer have the impetus to keep reading. What can you do about this? Simple!

Before you let the reader off the hook, hook them with a new line. It might look something like this.

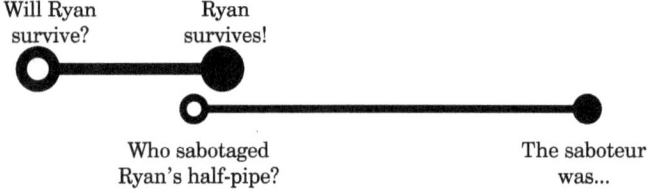

In fact you can overlap as many different tension lines as you want. A graph of your story could look something like this:

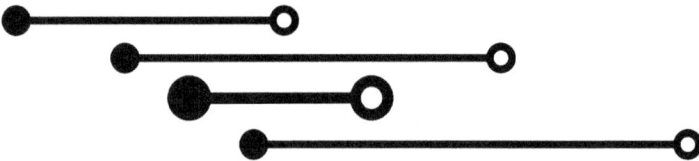

Remember each black dot is where you raise a question in the mind of the reader, and each white dot is where you give them the answer, and let them off the hook.

While you are writing your story take a note of where your tension lines start and finish. Make sure your reader is never off the hook!

Curiosity, anticipation and anxiety
The three cornerstones of suspense.

MY STORY

I intend to overlap a number of tension lines. The first one is, 'What has happened to Charli?'

By the time we find out where she is, there is another tension line. 'Charli is in terrible danger!'

Exercise

The night the ravens came, Sharyn was in her tent studying the bone fragments. She sighed and leaned back. She took out her bionic eye and polished it. It was hard to concentrate with the sounds coming from the strange object in the valley below.

She had tried to sleep earlier in the evening, but Reggie was snoring like a freight train in the tent next door. Later that night she would have been glad to have heard his snores. But you can't snore if you are no longer breathing.

A footstep sounded at the perimeter of the camp. She did not hear it, she saw it, on one of the sonic sensors that guarded the camp from intrusions by wild animals: bears; wolves; or miniature tigers. She reached for the alarm button but hesitated. Was it the professor or one of the porters out for a stroll? That small hesitation would prove extremely costly.

The footstep was followed by another, then another, not walking, running, right towards her tent. Now she did reach for her alarm but before she could press a button or shout a warning, the flap of her tent was flung back and a choking mist filled her nostrils and her mouth, stinging her eyes. She tried to scream but no sound emerged and as the stinging slowly faded, so did everything else.

-=============-

Reggie woke with his hand on his pistol, underneath the pillow. Something was very wrong. He was used to the sounds of the camp, but something was different. He rolled off his camp bed onto the floor, crouching on all fours. Silence. Too much silence. He opened the flap of his tent with the muzzle of the pistol, peering out. He could see nothing. He glanced back at the flashlight sitting on the camp table, but did not bother going back to get it. It was a fatal mistake.

He stepped outside and walked towards Sharyn's tent. Her light was on. She was up working. As always. Sharyn was convinced that they were getting close to solving the secret of the object in the valley.

It was then that he noticed the ravens. Three of them, black of wing and red of eye. Larger than any ravens he had ever seen. They were perched on the wire that led to the explosives truck. The birds seemed to be watching him. He waved his arms and they rose in a fluster of feathers, heading for nearby trees, but then whirling, turning. He realized, much too late, that they were coming for him.

BRIAN SAYS

Use a highlighter and mark every suspense technique you can find. Use different colours for different techniques.

I have used all of the techniques we have been discussing at least once, some twice, and some even more.

In fact I have really overdone it in this short passage. I have deliberately over-used the techniques just for the sake of the exercise.

Discuss with your writing buddy which of the examples create the greatest suspense and tension, and why.

Suspense Chart

Use this chart to plan the suspense techniques you will use to hook your readers.

Technique	Tension/Length	Description
(Example:) Hook	Medium/Long	Charli is missing. Where is she? Is she alive or dead?

The Promise of the Title

MY TITLES

Suspense starts with the title of your story. A good title will intrigue the reader. A great title will make them wonder about the contents of the book.

Here are a few of my titles, and what I think of them.

The Tomorrow Code ☺☺☺

A great title (thanks Jim Thomas!) The word 'tomorrow' implies the future and science fiction, which this book is. It also hints at the main idea of the book: messages from the future that arrive in Morse Code.

Brainjack ☺☺☺☺

There are two meanings to Brainjack. The word 'jack; can mean a electronic plug, like the one you plug your headhones into your phone. (In Brainjack, everyone plugs their brains directly into the internet). But the title also has the connotation of 'hijack.' IE a brainjack is a brain hijack, which is a very important theme of the story. I think this is the perfect title for this book.

The Project ☹☹☹☹

To me this title says nothing. The book is a fun, action-packed adventure, but you wouldn't know it from the title. This was not my original title, it got changed by the marketing department at my publisher. My idea for the title used reverse psychology. Let me explain: *The Project* is about a very rare, old book called *Leonardo's River*. This old book has the dubious distinction of being the most boring book in the world. But there is a reason why it is so boring. It hides a terrible secret. My original title for *The Project* was *The Most Boring Book in the World*. Now there's a title with a hook!

Battlesaurus: Rampage at Waterloo ☹

This is a great title, but unfortunately not for this book. The Battle of Waterloo is just one chapter in this book. Many people who have reviewed this book online have said that the book was not what they were expecting from the title. Fortunately they almost all say they were extremely pleasantly surprised.

Great Titles

Here are some wonderful titles, that promise the reader something or make them wonder something. If you haven't read these books, would you want to, based on the titles?

- **Where the Wild Things Are**
- **The Secret Garden**
- **Alexander and the Terrible, Horrible, No Good, Very Bad Day**
- **The Lion the Witch and the Wardrobe**
- **Charlie and the Chocolate Factory**
- **Danny the Champion of the World**
- **James and the Giant Peach**
- **The Cat in the Hat**
- **Cloudy with a chance of Meatballs**
- **Skulduggery Pleasant**

Each of these titles intrigues us in its own different way.

Now think about the title for your story. Write your ideas here. While you are writing your story, revisit these ideas occasionally, see which one stands out the most. Try them on your writing buddy. By the time you have finished writing your story, you should have a good idea of what you want the title to be.

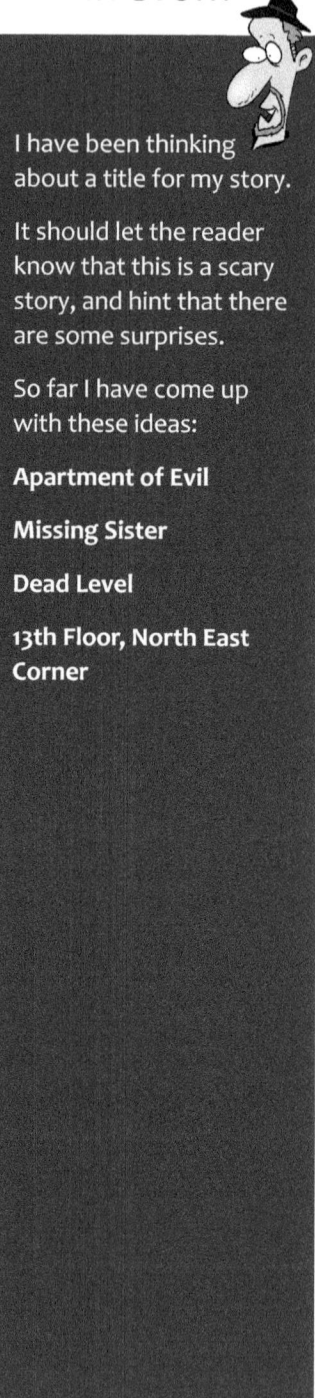

MY STORY

I have been thinking about a title for my story.

It should let the reader know that this is a scary story, and hint that there are some surprises.

So far I have come up with these ideas:

Apartment of Evil

Missing Sister

Dead Level

13th Floor, North East Corner

Rewriting ~~and Editing~~

We talked in *Word Warriors* (page 23) about editing.

Over the next two pages I will show you how I edit a story.

I have put the first page of my story, then an edited version of the same page.

Look at the changes. Discuss with your writing buddy the reason why I have made those changes, and whether you think they improved the story.

Then go and look at your own story.

Re-read page 23 from *Word Warriors.* Do all the things I have suggested there.

A published author will rewrite their story many, many times before they send it to a publisher. Then, if it is accepted, they will work with their editor and rewrite it many times more!

Your commitment to the excellence of your story will play a major role in determining whether your story is good enough to publish, and good enough for people to recommend to their friends.

QUOTES

I'm writing a first draft and reminding myself that Im simply shoveling sand into a box so that later I can build castles.
- *Shannon Hale*

Writing without revising is the literary equivalent of waltzing gaily out of the house in your underwear.
- *Patricia Fuller*

I'm not a very good writer, but I'm an excellent rewriter.
- *James Michener*

Only amateurs don't rewrite. It's in the rewriting that writers bring ALL their knowledge--basic craft, technique, style, organization, attitude, creative inspiration --to the work.
- *Gloria T. Delamar*

So the writer who breeds
more words than he needs,
is making a chore
for the reader who reads.
  - Dr Seuss

My Story - Original

"When was the last time you saw your sister alive?"
The question, once asked, cannot be un-asked even when the young policewoman realises what she has said and rephrases it quickly.

"When was the last time you saw your sister?"

I know the answer, because I have been thinking about it all morning. Tumbling it all over in my head till it is driving me insane.

The last time I saw Charli was when she went to bed. She was being naughty. Mum was getting stressed, so I went to sort it out. Most days, sorting family stuff out seems to be my job. I guess that's fair. I am the oldest.

Dad does it when he is here, which is like, never.

"She wouldn't go to sleep," I say. "Whenever I turned her light out, she turned it back on."

"How?" the other police-person asks. He is a big bear of a man with a short beard. He unwraps a stick of gum and starts chewing.

"There's a switch by the door, and one by the bed," I explain and the policeman nods.

"Did your mother not tell her off?" the policewoman asks.

"She was busy," I say.

I can't look at mum when I say that so I stare at the picture on the wall behind them. A painting of a young lady drinking a glass of soda through a straw. The glass is cold and frosted and it always makes me feel thirsty. Especially today. My throat is a desert. The gap where my missing tooth is feels dry and hard.

The police-people stay for another hour, asking lots of questions and examining Charli's room. Violet curtains, violet bedspread, a teddy-bear with a violet waistcoat. Quite neat and tidy, even the bed is made. But that's just Charli. She hates mess.

Mum seems relieved when the police-people leave. Not relieved that they are gone, but relieved that the problem is now out of her hands. Professionals are on the case.

I am not so convinced. They don't know where to start looking. They don't know anything.

They don't have a clue.

BRIAN SAYS

This is the same first page that you saw in *Word Warriors*.

I have repeated it here so you can compare it to the edited version on the next page.

To read the full story, go to:

www.writelikeanauthor.com/mystory

My Story - Edited

"When was the last time you saw your sister alive?"
The question, once asked, cannot be un-asked even when the young detective realises what she has said and rephrases it quickly.
"When was the last time you saw your sister?"
She fumbles for a pen in a pocket of her jacket as she says it, but I think she only does it so she doesn't have to meet my eyes. The other detective, a big bear of a man with a short beard, stares at my mother. He is wearing a dark suit, and looks like an FBI agent. Perhaps he wants people to think that.

I know the answer to the detective's question, because I have been thinking about it all morning. The memory pings around inside my head like a pinball, driving me crazy.

The last time I saw my sister was at bedtime. She was being naughty, refusing to turn her light out. Mum was getting stressed, so I went to sort it out. Most days, sorting family stuff out seems to be my job. I guess that's fair. I am the oldest.

Dad does it when he is here, but that is like, never.

"Charli wouldn't go to sleep," I say. "Whenever I turned her light out, she turned it back on."

"How?" the man asks. He unwraps a stick of gum and stares at it for a moment before sliding it into his mouth.

"There's another switch by the bed," I say.

"Do you often put your sister to bed?" the woman asks, writing it down as if it was a clue. But it isn't.

"I like to," I say. "It's kind of a big brother/little sister thing."

I can't look at mum when I say that so I stare at the picture on the wall behind them. It is a painting of a young lady drinking a glass of soda through a straw. I don't know where it came from, it was on the wall when we moved in. In the picture, the glass is cold and frosted and it always makes me feel thirsty. Especially today. My mouth is a desert. The gap where my tooth was feels dry and hard.

The detectives stay for another hour, most of it examining Charli's room. Violet curtains, violet bedspread, a teddy-bear with a violet waistcoat. They seem surprised at how neat and tidy it is. Even the bed is made. They make notes about that as if it was a clue too. But it's not a clue either. It's just Charli. She hates mess.

Mum seems relieved when the detectives leave. The problem is now out of her hands. Professionals are on the case.

I am not so convinced. They don't know where to start looking. They don't know anything.

They don't have a clue.

BRIAN SAYS

Most of the changes in this rewrite are quite subtle.

Some are to help establish the characters better, some are to create a more vivid image in the mind of the reader.

One specific change I made is the use of the word 'clue' twice before the final line on this page: *'they don't have a clue.'*

This is using **the rule of three**. The first two mentions of the word 'clue' build up to the third one, which is the important one. (Because it is the reason Jason sets out by himself to find his sister.)

Another important change was the short comment about the painting being on the wall when they moved in. I think it is important that this painting is part of the apartment, and not something they owned previously.

Where to from here?

Read!

Read books. Just for the fun of it. Then read it again, and look for the techniques you have learned.

The first time you read a story you are too busy experiencing the story to notice what the author is doing. Reading something a second time allows you to focus on the techniques used. Re-read stories you love and see if you can work out why you love them so much.

Read some stories you hate, and work out why they didn't appeal to you. Learn from good stories and from bad ones.

Write!

Practise your skills. Practise every day, even if it is for only a short time. If you only found half an hour each day to write, at the end of a week that's three and a half hours!

Review

Use these workbooks to review and remember what you have learned. Refer back to them often to refresh your memory.

Learn

Attend writing workshops and seminars, Including a *Write Like an Author* camp if you have not already attended one. Find what other writing workshops are available in your region or online.

You become a better writer the same way you get better at anything. By learning and by practising.

BRIAN SAYS

It is a long, hard road to becoming a published author, let alone a professional author, (someone who writes for a living.)

You need determination, perseverance and to believe in yourself if you are to have any chance of success.

Not everyone will make it. A lot of the people who read these words will give up, or just fall by the wayside.

I want you to be the one in a hundred who doesn't give up. Who never gives in, who doesn't quit.

Do you have what it takes to be a full-time professional author?

There's only one way to find out.

A professional writer is an amateur who didn't quit.

- Richard Bach

Quiz Answers

1. All children, except one, grow up
   Peter Pan by J.M. Barrie
   (Who is this child, and why don't they grow up?)

2. "Where's Papa going with that axe?" said Fern to her mother as they were setting the table for breakfast.
   Charlotte's Web by E.B. White
   (Where is Papa going with that axe!? And what is he going to do when he gets there?)

3. When the doorbell rings at three in the morning, it's never good news.
   Stormbreaker by Anthony Horowitz
   (What is the bad news that is about to be delivered?)

4. If you are interested in stories with happy endings, you would be better off reading some other book.
   A Series of Unfortunate Events: The Bad Beginning by Lemony Snicket
   (Why doesn't this book have a happy ending? What bad thing will happen? And why is the author advising us not to read the book?)

5. There is no lake at Camp Green Lake.
   Holes by Louis Sachar
   (Why is there no lake there, and why is that important?)

6. When Maddy started speaking Japanese, her mum took her to the doctor.
   Maddy West and the Tongue Taker by Brian Falkner
   (How did she just start speaking another language and why did her mum take her to the doctor?)

7. I felt her fear before I heard her screams.
   Vampire Academy by Richelle Mead
   (Whose fear? Why is she screaming?)

8. It was almost December, and Jonas was beginning to be frightened.
   The Giver by Lois Lowry
   (What is he frightened of?)

9. Look, I didn't want to be a half-blood.
   Percy Jackson and the Lightning Thief by Rick Riordan
   (What is a half-blood?)

10. He began his new life standing up, surrounded by cold darkness and stale, dusty air.
    The Maze Runner by James Dashner
    (Where is he? What new life?)

Course Notes:

www.ingramcontent.com/pod-product-compliance
Lightning Source LLC
LaVergne TN
LVHW081528060526
838200LV00045B/2043